LOON MAGIC
for Kids

LOON MAGIC

for Kids

by
Tom Klein

NorthWord
PRESS, INC

BOX 1360, MINOCQUA, WI 54548

*To the memory of Sigurd F. Olson (1899–1982)
who opened my mind and heart to the music of
the wilderness, and to his son, Sigurd. T. Olson,
who helped me understand loons.*

Copyright © 1989
NorthWord Press, Inc.

Designed by
Creative Services
Wausau, WI

Published by
NorthWord Press, Inc.
Box 1360
Minocqua, WI 54548

For a free catalog describing NorthWord's line of
nature books and gifts, call 1-800-336-5666

ISBN 1-55971-047-0

TABLE OF CONTENTS

INTRODUCTION

Loons are beautiful but bashful water birds. They live on clean, clear northern lakes amid deep green forests. Because they are so shy, loons are heard more often than seen. I love to listen to the long and lonely singing of loons. They sound strange and wild and exciting. These fascinating birds bring a special magic to the lake country – loon magic.

– *Tom Klein*

Loons and Where They Live

Loons eat, sleep and spend almost all their lives on the water. They are specially *adapted* for this kind of living. Their long, thin bodies move easily on and under the water. Big webbed feet push them along. Because they are fish eaters loons also have long, pointed bills which they use to capture *prey*.

Loons do most of their "fishing" by diving underwater. They can dive two hundred feet deep! Paddling with their feet and steering with their wings, loons chase and catch even the fastest minnows.

Adult loons spend the warm months of each year on northern lakes and rivers. There they make nests and raise their chicks. When autumn arrives, the chicks are fully grown. Before the northern lakes freeze, the mother, father and young loons all *migrate* south to the ocean coasts.

Loons are seen during the winter months off the Pacific coast of California, Oregon, Washington and even Alaska. They are also observed along the Atlantic coastal states from Maine south to Florida. Many loons also winter in the Gulf of Mexico near Texas, Louisiana and Mississippi.

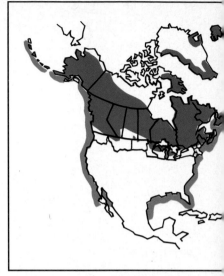

Common Loon

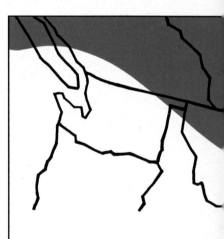

Detail of Common Loon breeding range

◼ Wintering Range
◼ Breeding Range

Red-throated Loon   Pacific Loon   Yellow-billed Loon

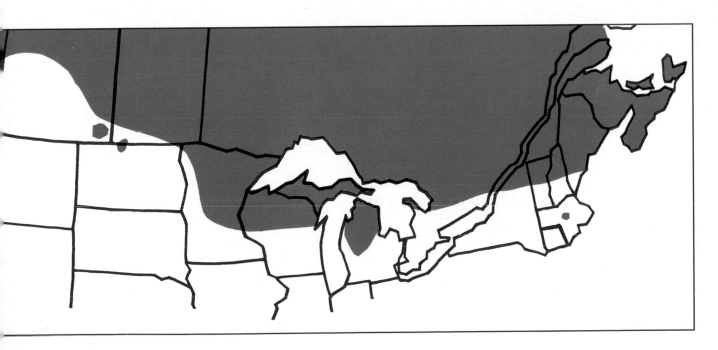

There are four different *species* of loons in the United States and Canada. They are not all the same size or color.

The red-throated loon is the smallest loon of all. It weighs only about four pounds. The yellow-billed loon weighs up to fourteen pounds. Three red-throated loons equal the weight of just one yellow-billed! That's why the species is called "king of the loon family."

The *plumage* of loon species varies too. The red-throated loon on the left does not look anything like the yellow-billed loon at the top of this page or the Pacific loon at the bottom.

All loons need privacy from humans. So, observe and enjoy loons from a distance. Never get too close to them or their nests. They may fly away and never return. Then their eggs won't hatch. Remember: without loons there can be no loon magic!

The Common Loon

The common loon is most often seen (and heard) by people in lake country. That's why, for most of us, it is our favorite loon species.

Common loons weigh about ten pounds. They measure around two and one half feet long. That's a pretty big bird! For a good idea of its size, look at the picture on the right hand page. See that tiny speck on the back of the loon's head? That's a mosquito!

Both male and female common loons have black and white plumage. And both have distinctive red eyes.

Why are the eyes red? Scientists believe that this color helps them see better when fishing underwater.

But the common loon is most famous for its mournful call. It has thrilled people for many years. Long ago, the writer Henry David Thoreau described it as "unearthly ... perhaps the wildest sound that is ever heard here, making the woods ring far and wide."

FOOD AND FEEDING

Loons often swim with their eyes open underwater. They are looking for prey. After spotting a fish, they dive and try to capture it in their bills. This is not always easy – even for loons!

Scientists have timed diving loons with stopwatches. One loon stayed underwater for over ten minutes! Most dives, however, last less than one minute.

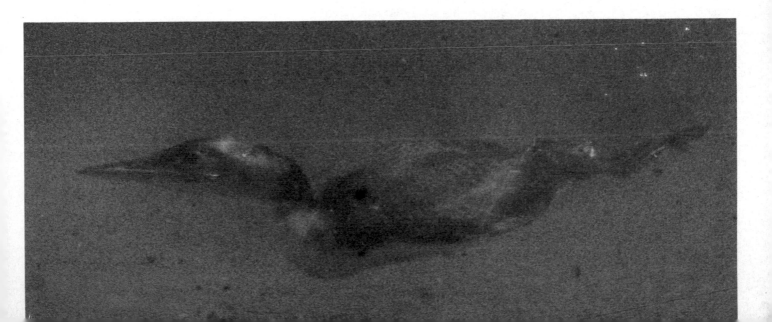

Captured fish are usually carried back to the surface. Loons do not chew fish. Instead, they swallow their food in one gulp. Loons have *elastic* throats. This allows them to swallow large prey. In fact, loons have been observed swallowing fish more than one half their own length.

Favorite foods of loons are small fish such as perch, bullhead and sunfish. But they will also eat frogs, crayfish and even leeches.

WATER DANCING

Loons have two interesting water "dances." Each dance has a different meaning.

The loon on the left page is trying to chase away other birds. He is splashing the water with his wings and kicking his feet so fast that he's walking on water!

The loon at right is very upset. He is doing the "penguin dance." With his wings folded against his body, he looks like another waterbird – the penguin. Loons do this dance when they have been disturbed by people coming too close to them.

The penguin dance is intended to scare enemies away from loon chicks. Sadly boaters sometimes come too close to loons. This starts the dancing. If the boaters are not smart enough to leave quickly, the loons may dance to exhaustion and die.

That's why people must learn to respect the rights of loons.

FLYING

Loons are excellent fliers – they can fly over 100 miles per hour! But they are not very good at all at taking off. In fact, loons must run across the water for about a quarter of a mile before taking flight.

Loons also *ascend* very slowly. Taking off from a small lake, a loon must circle several times before lifting high enough to clear the shoreline tree tops.

PREENING

Preening is what loons do to take care of their feathers. It is an important part of their daily routine. Using only their bills, loons busily clean and adjust feathers and remove bugs. They even oil their feathers using a special gland near the tail.

A clean loon is a healthy and happy loon!

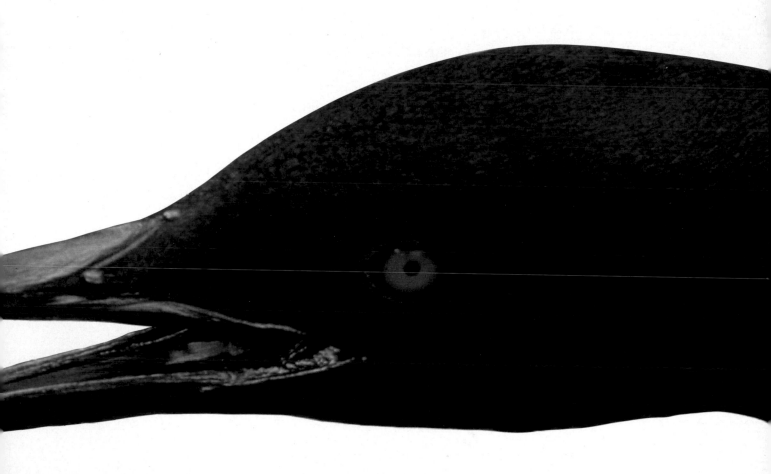

Nest Building and Nesting

After spring mating, male and female loons must build a nest. These are usually located in grass along the lake shoreline. Loons may use the same nest sites year after year.

Loons don't build very fancy nests. They usually just pick up pieces of nearby weeds and grass in their bills and plunk them down in a pile. The loon at right is doing just that.

Both the male and female loon take turns sitting on the eggs. This keeps the eggs warm so the young chicks inside will grow. The egg-sitting process is called *incubation.*

Loons are good parents. They turn the eggs with their bills to ensure even warmth. Day after day the parents incubate the eggs. Not even violent storms or nearby predators will force them to leave the nest.

Then, after about one month of incubation, the eggs begin to hatch!

After hatching, loon chicks stay in the nest only long enough to rest and dry off. Soon they are in the water and swimming with their parents.

RAISING CHICKS

Loon chicks are dependent upon their parents for food, warmth and safety. Because the hungry chicks cannot dive and catch their own fish, the parents feed them. During their first few days of life, the chicks are fed only little bits of fish. Next come live minnows. After a week or so they are diving after their own fish – but not catching many!

Swimming too long in the cold water can be harmful to young chicks. That's why they frequently ride on their parents' back. These "free rides" also keep the chicks safe from underwater predators like snapping turtles, northern pike and muskies.

This little chick is trying to sing like his mom and dad. The sound, however, is barely more than a peep!

As we have already learned, the chick will be fully grown by autumn. Before winter he will fly south to the warm waters of an ocean coast. He may spend up to three years there.

But one spring morning he will appear on a quiet lake of his native northland. Fully grown, tested by the rigors of survival, he will tilt back his head and give song. This time the sound will not be a peep. It will be a loud and thrilling song that makes the forest ring far and wide!

Maybe you will be lucky enough to hear him. If so, you will know that this lake has been touched by a special magic – loon magic.

Parent Participation Page

1. WHAT AGE CAN INDIVIDUAL LOONS ATTAIN? 15 – 30 years.

2. HOW OLD IS THE LOON AS A SPECIES? Loons are the oldest and most primitive living bird, reaching back about 50 million years – nearly to the age of the dinosaurs.

3. DO LOONS MATE FOR LIFE? Maybe. Data is insufficient. However, since the bond is not strong enough to keep the loon pair together through migration and wintering, it's likely not strong enough to insure lifelong partnership. Yet the strong fidelity to the nest site lends possibility to such bonding.

4. HOW OFTEN DO LOONS COME ASHORE? Only to nest. Loons are all but immobile on land. They cannot stand and walk erect like a duck or goose – the legs are too far back on their bodies. Instead, when on land, loons must awkwardly push themselves along with their feet.

Ocassionally loons will land on wet roads, thinking them rivers. In such cases, the birds are completely helpless and unable to take flight. Several years ago near Minocqua, Wisconsin, 16 migrating loons mistook a local highway for a likely roosting river. After some bumpy landings, the helpless loons were spotted by a quick-thinking motorist who blocked the road. The birds were then gathered up and driven to the Minocqua Wildlife Rehabilitation Center. There they were treated for various abrasions to feet and bills then released in a nearby lake. From there the loons completed their migration without further apparent mishap.

5. DO LOONS NEST ON THE OCEAN? There are no reports of loons having nested on the coast. However, loons are commonly sighted off the coast of Maine and New Hampshire during the breeding season. These birds are either traveling from inland lakes to feed or are unmated loons without inland breeding territories.

6. ARE LOONS ENDANGERED? Officially, no. Common loons do not appear on the U.S. Fish and Wildlife Service list of Endangered or Threatened species. In some parts of their range however, the loon is in trouble. Many states list the loon as endangerd, rare or threatened.

7. ARE LOON EGGSHELLS GETTING THIN? Pesticides, especially DDT, have created such problems for many birds, including eagles, ospreys and peregrine falcons. While current loon eggshells are about 10% thinner than those from the pre-DDT era, loons continue to reproduce successfully.

8. DO LOONS LAY MORE THAN ONE SET OF EGGS PER SEASON? Yes, if the original eggs are lost to predators, loons may lay eggs a second or even a third time. Conversely, loons do not necessarily lay eggs every year. Studies indicate that one in every four years or so they'll take a year off from nesting.

9. WHAT IS THE SURVIVAL RATE OF HATCHED CHICKS? Unusually high among members of the bird world. Due to excellent parental care, it is estimated at about 50%.

10. WHERE CAN WE FIND OUT MORE ABOUT LOONS? The North American Loon Fund (NALF) exists to support and coordinate its affiliate groups (listed below) with financial resources, technical data and educational materials. Its offices are located in Meredith, New Hampshire.

North American Loon Fund
Main St., Humiston Building
Meredith, New Hampshire 03853
603/279-6163

Affiliated Loon Groups

Common Loon Protection Project
Maine Audubon Society
118 Old Route 1
Falmouth, ME 04105

Loon Survey Project
Vermont Institute of Natural Science
Woodstock, VT 05091

Loon Preservation Committee
Audubon Society of New Hampshire
Main Street
Meredith, NH 03253

Audubon Society of New York
8 Wade Road
Latham, NY 12110

Michigan Loon Preservation Association
c/o Michigan Audubon Society
409 West E. Avenue
Kalamazoo, MI 49007

Minnesota Loon Appreciation Committee
506 Torrey Building, 314 W. Superior St.
Duluth, MN 55802

Wisconsin Project Loon Watch
Sigurd Olson Environmental Institute
Northland College
Ashland, Wisconsin 54806

Montana Loon Project
7 East Mason #2
Bozeman, MT 59715

Loon Lake Association
P.O. Box 75
Loon Lake, WA 99148

Ontario Lakes Loon Survey
Long Point Bird Observatory
Port Rowan, Ontario
NOE 1MO

INDEX:
NEW WORDS FROM 'LOON MAGIC FOR KIDS'

The words below also appeared in the text in italicized type. The page number on which each word first appeared is listed after each definition. After reading the definition, you may wish to turn back to the text page and review the new word within a sentence.

ADAPTED. To adjust or conform to a certain way of living – Page 9.

ASCEND. To rise slowly upward – Page 28.

CAMOUFLAGE. A coloring disguise that hides an object from view – Page 35.

ELASTIC. The ability of something to stretch then return to its original shape – Page 22.

INCUBATION. Sitting on eggs so body warmth may hatch them – Page 36.

MIGRATE. To move from one area to another – Page 10.

PLUMAGE. All the feathers on a birds body – Page 13.

PREY. Fish or animals that are eaten by predators – Page 9.

SPECIES. Animals with similar features and habitats that can also interbreed – Page 13.

PHOTOGRAPHIC CREDITS: Bob Baldwin, ii, 14, 21, 40; Adam Bayer, 38; Denver Bryan, 38; R.C. Burke, iv, vi; Daniel J. Cox, 8, 19, 27, 42, 43; Glenn Irwin, 24, 31; Edgar Jones, 13, 29; Tom klein, vii, 26; S. Kraseman (DRK photo), 28; Tom Magelson (DRK photo), 20, 30; Tom Martinson, Cover; Peter Roberts, 17, 30, 33, 37; W. E. Ruth, 45; Lynn Rogers, 18, 25, 34, 35, 39, Back Cover; Tom Walker, 12; Mark Wallner, 23.